THE NATIONAL READ A BOOK DAY: A trip to the beginning and the significance of reading.

Michael Kante

TABLE OF CONTENT

CHAPTER 1: NATIONAL HISTORY BOOK READING DAY

CHAPTER 2: American History Of National Reading Day

CHAPTER 3: National Reading Day: Why it's important to instill a love of reading in children.

CHAPTER 4: The Benefits Of Reading

CHAPTER 5: Quotes On Reading

CHAPTER 1: NATIONAL HISTORY BOOK READING DAY

On September 6, National Read a Book Day encourages all book enthusiasts to indulge in their pastimes guilt-free. Books open up new worlds for us to explore and take us on thrilling journeys. In ways that no other kind of media can equal, they may challenge our conceptions of the human condition. National Read a Book Day exhorts us to flip the pages and escape the cacophony in a world overrun by technology.

While it is thought that National Read a Book Day started in the US, nothing is known about the day's earlier existence. But one thing is certain: Americans like reading! And because 81% of us believe we don't read as much as we would want, many people are happy to see this day. Therefore, today is the ideal day to set aside some time to read everything on our "to read" list.

The success of book clubs is evidence of our enduring passion of reading. Women's Bible studies go all the way back to the sixteen hundreds. However, reading has become considerably more sociable in recent years, thanks in large part to Oprah Winfrey's Book Club. Beginning in 1996, Oprah's Book Club suggested 70 books, resulting in sales of more than $55 million, and is credited with encouraging millions of people to read.

In the last 12 months, more than 74% of Americans have read at least one book. Yes, the activity of life interferes with our efforts to read since there are so many other things vying for our attention. Fortunately, reading on the move is now much simpler thanks to technological platforms. Nowadays, around 20% of books are read on electronic platforms. Grab the book at the top of your stack, download it, and start reading, whichever format you want!

In India, the 19th of June is observed as National Reading Day in memory of P.N. Panicker, a Keralite educator. It wasn't until 1996 that this festival of reading got going. However, over time, it has developed into a significant movement with many members who are happy, educating themselves, consuming, and enjoying the habit of reading.

In Kerala, Puthuvayil Narayana Panicker is credited with starting the drive for public libraries. After his passing on June 19, 1995, National Reading Day was observed in his honor on June 19th, 1996. Vayana Varam, or "reading week," is also observed by the Kerala Ministry of Education from June 19 to June 25.

National Reading Day - Contributions of P.N. Panicker

Panicker, a teacher in his village, established the Sanadana Dalman Library in 1926. Twenty years later, in 1945, he served as the president of the Travancore Library Association, which included 47 neighborhood libraries under the Thiruvithaamkoor Granthasala Sangham. Emphasizing the value of local education and reading was the fundamental motivation for the establishment of these libraries. The club's motto, "Read and Grow," captures the value of reading in daily life.

When Kerala became a state in 1956, the organization changed its name to Kerala Granthsala Sangham (SGS). Nearly 6,000 libraries are now part of Panicker's network. In 1975, the SGS was given the esteemed

Krupsakaya Award by UNESCO. Before the state government took control of it in 1977, Panicker served as the organization's general secretary for 32 years. It then changed its name to the Kerala State Library Council and added financing and democratic processes.

Panicker made the decision to form Kerala's Kerala Association for Non-Formal Education and Development (KANFED) after the state's purchase of SGS. A mission to increase literacy in Kerala was started as a result of KANFED, which also emphasized the value of education in rural regions.

CHAPTER 2: American History Of National Reading Day

"You will learn more stuff the more you read. You'll go further and discover more things the more you know. Theodor Seuss

September is recognized as National Reading Month each year. The beginning of this is marked by "Read Across America Day" on September 6, which also happens to be the birthday of Dr. Seuss, one of the most well-known writers of children's books in history. It is customary to tell tales and anecdotes about his fantastic characters, and this is the best approach to pique kids' interests in reading.

In order to make reading more enjoyable and participatory for kids, Read Across America Day is primarily a reading campaign that encourages everyone to read. Reading has a crucial part in forming who we are, from the early years when our character is formed through maturity when we turn to books to escape the monotony of everyday life. It is more important than ever to encourage kids to read in the age of smartphones and tablets.

Since 1998, the National Education Association (NEA) has been in charge of the Read Across America program. They are primarily concerned with improving public education. With the help of activities held in libraries, schools, book clubs, and communities, reading has been encouraged throughout the country. Additionally, educators and organization leaders may sign the pledge and submit their proposal on the NEA website. In this approach, the event attracts more interest and attendees.

However, celebrities also have a role in encouraging the next generation of readers, in addition to educators and librarians. Since the declaration of the day, actors, athletes, and other well-known people have utilized their platforms to promote the delights of reading. Some have even taken part in children's reading circles to draw attention to this cause.

March has been declared as National Reading Month in celebration of Dr. Seuss' birthday, encouraging people of all ages to read every day.

Regardless of age, reading is enjoyable and has numerous advantages. It's important for both professional and educational growth. Additionally, it has both short-term and long-term positive effects on one's health, including improvements in memory, cognitive ability, vocabulary, empathy, and stress levels.

America's Charities is happy to celebrate the following changemakers that we are honored to name our members in recognition of #NationalReadingMonth:

It takes more than just bricks and mortar to create prosperous futures, according to Arlington Housing Corporation (AHC Inc.), a not-for-profit provider of affordable housing communities for low-income families and people in the mid-Atlantic area. Via social assistance and year-round educational programs including after-school reading activities, teen tutoring, college and career preparation, and a summer camp to minimize learning loss, AHC is fostering stability and opportunity through its award-winning Resident Services program.

Reading Is Essential - Reading Is Fundamental is dedicated to creating a literate America by igniting a love of reading in all children, offering impactful material, and involving communities in the solution to provide every kid the fundamental foundation for success. Their impact strategy is based on fostering a culture of reading for the kids they work with by giving them access to books of their choosing, as well as chances for interaction with the teachers, parents, and other adults who are responsible for raising them. To foster a lifetime love of reading, Reading Is Fundamental offers free books to kids countrywide and actively involves communities, parents, and kids in reading and motivating events.

CHAPTER 3: National Reading Day: Why it's important to instill a love of reading in children.

In the midst of lockdowns, technology let individuals and companies flourish. The digital era had arrived as 2020 arrived with its own set of challenges, affecting every aspect of our lives, including how we work, study, and communicate.

Many devoted readers used the downtime to catch up on their reading lists, and a large number of new readers started discovering the fascinating world of books, whether they were digital or traditional. Whatever the format, it was encouraging to see the growth of reading habits, which in turn helped individuals improve their knowledge, mindfulness, and, in many instances, just their ability to unwind.

Numerous studies demonstrate that reading for at least an hour each day significantly increases productivity, lowers stress levels, and promotes sleep. In case you need more motivation to start reading that unfinished book in this always-on, digital world, here are some more:

Enhances mental health

The global epidemic marked a turning point in raising awareness of the value of mental health and wellbeing. Additionally, reading may significantly enhance mental health when it is encouraged early on. Reading on a daily basis may not only maintain the mind strong and agile but also provide a haven of peace.

Improves cognition and focus

We may now easily access texts from anywhere on the globe thanks to digital reading technologies, which also allow us to broaden our range of educational and recreational opportunities. A simple approach to reading literature in many languages and formats is now audiobooks. Although it is now simpler to obtain the content, attention spans are still a problem in the modern world. Reading, whether on or offline screens, is a fantastic technique to increase concentration span, creativity, and imagination. There is no denying that reading piques one's curiosity and inspires a desire to lead.

Improves communication abilities

Communication skills are important in any industry. The printed word's influence only grows as communications shift more and more toward the internet. Reading is the most crucial first step if you want to distinguish out from the crowd with your writing and speaking abilities. There is substantial evidence to suggest that reading, particularly when done as a young child, not only increases vocabulary but also helps writing abilities. Your vocabulary will improve as you read more widely because it will be easier for you to put words and phrases into context and use them effectively.

Energizes the brain

Reading assignments may help the social media generation concentrate better and exercise their brains since they have shorter attention spans than previous generations. According to a study from Stanford University, close literary reading challenges your brain to do a variety of sophisticated cognitive tasks, while pleasure reading improves blood flow to many parts of the brain. This mental exercise is essential to enhancing learning capacity and stimulating the intellect. So let's make a vow to read more, read better, and read more often.

The American writer Ernest Hemingway once said, "There Is No Friend As Loyal As A Book." Books stimulate the imagination, provide comfort through difficult times, and expand the mind.

Because reading expands one's mind to new experiences and offers new avenues for knowledge, it is fundamentally linked to professional success.

Reading may improve your writing and speaking abilities. By tailoring how you read, reading abilities may advance you and assist you in achieving your goals. You Can Improve Your Reading Process And Achieve Your Goal If You Pick The Right Reading Skill.

Use extensive reading skills if you want to read for pleasure. There is no expectation placed on the reader in this passage, and context may be used to interpret word meanings. For instance, you would be able to deduce that the meaning of tread has to do with walking after reading the sentence, "Tread Softly Because You Tread On My Dreams."

The most often used reading technique is intensive reading. Here, you completely listen to every word and comprehend everything. While it would take you a lot longer to read using this method, the text would be much more thoroughly understood.

Critical reading is a different reading skill that aids in analyzing and challenging the assumptions made in the text. You Are Able To Reach Your Conclusions Because Of It.

Skimming is a method used to quickly scan information. For instance, reading a book first before buying it. Sometimes while reading, you just scan a certain section. This ability is known as scanning.

You Can Get The Most Out Of Reading If You Pick The Right Approach. For instance, you shouldn't skim anything that you need to review for a report. Similar to this, you may not want to use your skill at extensive reading for a subject that you find uninteresting.

CHAPTER 4: The Benefits Of Reading

Reading improves our lives in a number of ways:

Conditioning Your Mind

Reading is beneficial since it uses different parts of your brain. Reading helps you develop your comprehension skills and analytical skills. It piques your imagination and activates your memory centers. It aids with memory retention and stabilizes your emotions.

The Strengthening Of Mental Muscles Is The Importance Of A Reading Habit. One of the best mental exercises is reading. It has been shown that regular mental stimulation may delay the onset of diseases like

Alzheimer's and dementia and may even prevent them. Reading Maintains A Flexible And Young Mind.

Reading Comprehension's Function in Communication

In his book The Medici Effect, Swedish-American author Frans Johansson explains how creativity is intersectional. Ideas that originate in one medium or industry might serve as an example to another.

Writing and reading both functions similarly. Reading Enhances the Flow and Style of Your Writing. Taking inspiration from other writers helps writers hone their craft. Lack of reading makes it impossible to be a good writer. The renowned author Stephen King is said to always have a book with him. Even while eating, he reads.

The development of your oratory abilities is a crucial aspect of reading comprehension in communication. Reading teaches you new vocabulary and viewpoints. It aids in constructing clearer sentences and stronger language. You get a stronger command of the language as a result. These are all essential for effective speaking.

Discovering Yourself

Newer worlds may be accessed via books. They have the power to broaden your perspective, mold your outlook on people and life, and expose you to fresh perspectives on day-to-day experiences.

Reading Has Many Benefits, One Of Which Is That It Helps You Develop Your Identity. You choose who you want to become through reading. You Steal Ideas From Fictional Characters That You Love. Reading Sherlock Holmes, for instance, can encourage you to train as a detective or just sharpen your observational and analytical skills.

Developing Your Reading Skills

People Who Read Well Are Admired. The Phrase "Well-Read" Is Frequently Used To Describe An Intelligent, Wise Person.

Books were the only sources of knowledge and information prior to the advent of the Internet. The Collective Wisdom Of Our Times Is Found In Books. You will learn more about the world and its inhabitants the more you read. One of the many advantages of reading is that it advances your knowledge of the world.

Maintaining Peace and Amusement

Books are a great way to escape from the real world. They are able to make you feel better when you are unhappy, inspire you when you are depressed, and even keep you company while everyone else is busy.

Reading has the advantage of calming your body and mind. When you read, your energy levels replenish much more quickly. The best way to end the day peacefully is to read. Even better, it could help you fall asleep more quickly.

Benefits of Reading

The aforementioned details highlight how crucial it is to keep up a reading routine. Here Are A Few More Advantages Of Regular Reading:

enhances your capacity for thought and analysis

Sometimes after reading a book, you realize the plot has flaws in it. Before the book reveals who the murderer is, you already know. Reading Makes Your Mind Work Faster for Some Reason.

Your analytical and critical thinking skills are sent into overdrive when you read. Every book turns into a puzzle that your mind tries to solve. It keeps raising its rating with each book.

The real world may also benefit from these same abilities. The mind of a reader is trained to pick up on minute details. It connects the dots and brings the puzzle pieces together. It Has Greater Skill In Pattern Recognition And Puzzle Solving. It gains the ability to better synthesize knowledge. This topic is covered in the post-reading module of the course on reading deeply offered by Harappa Education.

Enables you to block out noise

Short attention spans are the norm as interruptions and activity fill our lives on a constant basis.

The Management Of Your WhatsApp Messages Is Required Of You Checking your email while interacting with your coworkers is simultaneous. Such multitasking impairs concentration and productivity.

However, reading a book focuses all of your attention. It is impossible to overstate the value of reading in the digital age. It may be the last remaining option for enhancing focus and attention.

Enhances Language Learning

One of the best ways to learn a new language or improve your command of an existing one is by reading. Additionally, stories help you learn much faster.

Contextual learning is one of the most natural ways to understand the meaning of words and expand your vocabulary. Additionally, it aids in learning common terms.

Developing Relationships

Books Can Help You Bond With New People And Be A Great Conversation Starter.

Because of their knowledge, readers may easily become the center of attention and have a variety of stories to share or topics to discuss. They are well-liked for their capacity to critically analyze problems objectively.

Keeps You Stable

Reading is a continuous humility exercise. You become more aware of how little reading you have done as you do more.

That serves as a reminder of how much work remains. Each book serves as a reminder of your knowledge's limitations.

Readers Are More Accepting And Friendly To Others. They are always helpful since they are aware that they are also still developing.

Reading is an essential habit because of its advantages. A book has a wide range of potential uses. It may serve as a map if you get lost. When you feel alone, it might be your companion.

While These Advantages Are Amazing, Reading Deeply Needs Professional Assistance. The Reading Deeply course from Harappa Education, which helps you raise your reading quotient, teaches you all there is to know about it. To begin your reading journey, sign up right now.

CHAPTER 5: Quotes On Reading

The eighth of September is International Literacy Day, did you know that? I didn't till yesterday, which cost me the opportunity to have some cake. (I'm always seeking an excuse to indulge in cake.)

I completely agree that there should be a designated day to honor reading (and indulge in cake), but I also believe that literacy should be a top priority all year long. Books and reading have always been at the core of my attempts to foster the minority language as a teacher and, more recently, as the father of bilingual children.

Reading has a huge impact on language development in all of its forms, and in today's world, it's impossible to exaggerate how important reading is to every area of life.

I've gathered 43 of my favorite quotations about the value and power of reading to assist make my argument. Take a huge slice of cake and follow along as I read...

1. A book is a present you can unwrap repeatedly. — Garrison Keillor

2. Literacy serves as a conduit from despair to hope. — Kofi Annan

3. You will always be free once you can read. — Frederic Douglas

4. Any book that encourages a youngster to develop a reading habit and make reading a need for him is beneficial to him. — Maya Angelou

5. There are only kids who haven't discovered the proper book; there is no such thing as a kid who despises reading. — Frank Serafini

6. Parents teach their children to read as they sit on their laps. Emma Buchwald

7. Reading to children is one of the finest gifts people can provide to their children and to society. Sagan, Carl

8. You could possess untold material riches, including gold and jewel-encrusted chests. I can never be richer than you are. My mother used to read to me. —Strickland Gillian

9. Reading shouldn't be seen as a work or obligation for kids. They should be given it as a priceless gift. Katherine DiCamillo

10. Somewhere in the globe, a door opens to let in more light whenever you read a fantastic book. —Vera Nazarian

11. A book is a man's closest companion, second only to a dog. It's too dark to read inside a dog. — Groucho Marx

12. In a child's life, books are indispensable. —May Ellen Chase

13. Learning to read is like starting a fire; each word written down is a spark. Vincent Hugo

14. It is not enough to only educate youngsters how to read; we also need to provide them with material that is worthwhile. Something that will challenge their imaginations, aid them in making sense of their own lives, and inspire them to interact with others who lead quite different lives from their own. Kathy Patterson

15. You will experience a new birth when you begin to read.

and you won't again feel alone quite like before. Ruther Godden

16. C.S. Lewis once said, "We read to know we are not alone."

17. Children who learn to read fluently and effectively start to fly into whole new worlds with the same ease that young birds do. —William James

18. There are several little methods to broaden your child's horizons. The finest of all is a love of literature. — Jackie Kennedy

19. A love of reading is the finest gift. —Elizabeth Hardwick

20. The days we spent reading a beloved book were maybe the only days of our childhood that we really lived. Proust, Marcel

21. Children's fairy stories serve as stepping stones throughout life, pointing the route through adversity and difficulty. Fairy tales are valuable because they give us hope that good really does triumph over evil and that even the grimmest reality can result in a Happily Ever After, rather than because they provide a brief literary escape from reality. Do not undervalue that gift of hope. It has the ability to overcome sadness and

despair, dispel the gloom in life's valleys, and utter "One more time" in the face of failure. Hope is what breathes life into dreams and transforms them into fairy tales. — L.R. Knost

22. Continue reading. Faulkner, William

www.ingramcontent.com/pod-product-compliance
Lightning Source LLC
LaVergne TN
LVHW020536160826
845677LV00015B/4085
* 9 7 9 8 3 5 3 4 2 9 1 9 7 *